It's Hard

TO DO

Good

Kenneth H. McGaffic

It's Hard to Do Good

Trilogy Christian Publishers
A Wholly Owned Subsidiary of Trinity Broadcasting Network
2442 Michelle Drive, Tustin, CA 92780

Trilogy Christian Publishing/ TBN and colophon are trademarks of Trinity Broadcasting Network. For information about special discounts for bulk purchases, please contact Trilogy Christian Publishing.

Manufactured in the United States of America

Trilogy Disclaimer: The views and content expressed in this book are those of the author and may not necessarily reflect the views and doctrine of Trilogy Christian Publishing or the Trinity Broadcasting Network.

10 9 8 7 6 5 4 3 2 1
Library of Congress Cataloging-in-Publication Data is available.

B-ISBN#: 978-1-63769-154-0
E-ISBN#: 978-1-63769-155-7 (e-book)

DEDICATION

Whoso findeth a wife findeth a good thing, and obtaineth favour of the Lord.

—Proverbs 18:22, KJV

This book is dedicated to Linda, my lovely wife for more than four decades. I better interject here, we met and married young. One of my favorite sayings is when I met Linda, I saw a diamond in the rough. She is quick to respond, "when I saw you, I saw a lump of coal." God's been chipping away on both of us now for many years. Linda is a great wife, mother, business partner and most of all, my best friend.

It's also dedicated to my two beautiful daughters, Erin and Kelly. I don't know if a dad could be prouder than I am of my daughters. They love Jesus and are now wives and mothers of their own families. But to me, they'll always be the little girls I tucked in bed every night asking me to read them a book. After all these years, I think I can still recite their favorite books from memory.

ACKNOWLEDGMENT

This book may have never came to print without the help of Matt Ciampaglione, a longtime employee and friend. Matt was the one who deciphered my "chicken scratch" and put it in typed form. I'm sure I could have eventually typed it myself, but my thoughts move quicker than my fingers. It might have been different if in high school had I signed up for typing instead of a food class. The allure of warm chocolate chip cookies won out over the thought of banging away on manual typewriters. I think it still would today.

CONTENTS

What would a life be
If it was only to live
A selfish desire to
Get more than give
But to share one's life daily
With those who have needs
Is to be a true follower
Of the shepherd that leads.

—Kenneth H. McGaffic

PREFACE

It's Hard to Do Good

It was a typical early spring morning in western Pennsylvania. The weather was unpredictable at best. As I was driving home from my workout at the local YMCA, I saw a few young teens headed to school walking in the rain. As I like to say, "I can hit the school with a nine iron (on a good day) from my front yard." These kids were nearly a mile away from the school. The thought entered my mind to offer these kids a ride to school. It would beat them being soaked for the first class of the day. But just as quickly as the thought entered my head, I quickly dismissed it. A middle-aged man offering to give kids a ride to school, in our society, just doesn't work anymore. Good intentions can quickly bring misery and heartache through false perceptions. As I continued on my way home I thought, *it's a shame that it's hard to do good today.* Spontaneous acts of charity need to be weighed against legal, cultural, and governmental consequences, often in a split second.

Despite this, the scriptures command us to "do good"! I confess I don't have all the answers. I probably have more questions than answers. But from these thoughts, this book was birthed.

CHAPTER 1

Hero to Zero

Owning an advertising agency, and co-owning a nationally recognized craft festival with my wife, as well as being a minister, has given me a unique insight into the workings of human nature. One of my favorite sayings is, "You can go from hero to zero in a matter of seconds." What does that mean? Well, whether in your personal life, business world, or ministry, one mistake or misspoken word can ruin your life or career. It's become more apparent today in our "cancel culture". Though the saying is not original, it's reality.

> Now when he was in Jerusalem at the passover,
> in the feast day, many believed in his name, when
> they saw the miracles which he did. But Jesus did
> not commit himself unto them, because he knew
> all men, and needed not that any should testify of
> man: for he knew what was in man.
>
> —John 2:23-25, KJV

These verses tell us many believed in Jesus when they saw the miracles He performed. Jesus was well aware of the fickleness of people, so His actions didn't depend on whether they were on His bandwagon. His motivation was simply to do the will of the Father. It should speak volumes to us.

We've all heard stories of how a good Samaritan (I talk more about him in later chapters) helps out someone who is in a desperate situation, saves their lives, or saves them from greater injury, and ends up being sued when all the dust settles by the one who they went to the aid of.

Ask most police officers which is the most difficult call to go on. More often than not they'll say a domestic call. A former state police officer relayed a story to me that happened to him very early in his career. He and another officer went to a home to investigate a domestic disturbance between a husband and his wife. The wife had obviously been beaten (apparent by her bruises). But when the officers attempted to arrest the husband, the wife pulled a gun on them. The former officer stated he narrowly escaped a quick end to his career.

I've seen pastors who loved their flocks and invested their lives for the members of their congregations only to have their good efforts spoken against by the very people they were laying down their lives to help.

> Let not then your good be evil spoken of.
>
> —Romans 14:16, KJV

Unfortunately, it's human nature to be self-centered, putting yourself first at the expense of others. Even when an act of kindness is done on your behalf. A "self-centerer" screams, "I want more, I need more, it's about me! Thanks for what you did for me a minute ago, but that was then and this is now." With all this in mind, what should our attitude be as we try to do good? It's simply, "Do all things as unto God and not unto men."

I remember an instance many years ago when our church was preparing the parking lot for paving. A few brothers were working when we pulled up in our car. Heading into the building to fulfill a task, I heard one of the volunteers complaining, loud enough that we could hear, that they were out there sweating while others didn't care. The instant I heard it, I saw in my mind's eye a bag of gold dust the complaining brother would have received as an eternal reward for his efforts. Now the bag had a hole in it, all the gold dust was draining out and he lost everything by the words he spoke.

It's great to get a pat on the back for doing good, but if that's your motivation, you will be severely disappointed.

> And whatsoever ye do, do it heartily, as to the
> Lord, and not unto men; Knowing that of the
> Lord ye shall receive the reward of the inheritance:
> for ye serve the Lord Christ.
>
> —Colossians 3:23-24, KJV

> That thine alms may be in secret: and thy Father
> which seeth in secret himself shall reward thee
> openly.
>
> —Matthew 6:4, KJV

If you are helping someone and expecting something in return, you are doing *business*, not *kindness*.

Whether on the job, in our family setting, neighborhood, or church, resentments or bitterness can be stopped before it starts by seeing our reward comes from the Father and not man.

I worked in a steel mill in the wire department (which I mention later on in the book). As a wire drawer, we not only earned an hourly wage, but also a commission on the work we put out.

Certain wires drawn paid a higher payout than others. So it was common for workers to slow the production down to a snail's pace on jobs that were low paying. "Why work hard if you're not going to get rewarded for it?"

Even as a young believer, I had the understanding I wasn't working for J & L Steel, I was working for God. So regardless how much I could earn from the commission, I worked at the same pace. Often my fellow workers would wander past my machine with palms down encouraging me to slow down. It didn't phase me. I wasn't working for them or the company, I knew God was a good paymaster and if I was faithful to do things unto Him, I would be blessed.

The steel mill is no longer there. Many of those who encouraged me to slow down lost their livelihoods. Who knows, it may have been different if the company and union worked together unto God.

We must look past the person, business, or ministry and see Christ. Jesus said when you've done it to the least of these, you've done it unto me.

Thanks is not always forthcoming by those who we've done good to … but how God views it is what really counts.

CHAPTER 2

The Good Samaritan

Did you know that most states in the United States, and Canada, have Good Samaritan laws? These laws offer limited protection for someone who attempts to help a person in distress. Good Samaritan laws are written to encourage someone who sees an emergency situation to step up to the plate and get involved without fearing that they might be sued if their actions inadvertently cause more harm than good.

Seconds are critical in an emergency. A bystander's help can make the difference between life and death before emergency professionals arrive. In fact, there are laws in some states that require bystanders to act in some limited capacity. Naturally, common sense needs to prevail. Running into a burning building, or trying to help someone who fell and may have injured their neck without the proper equipment, may not be the best course of action.

That brings us to the Parable of the Good Samaritan.

> And Jesus answering said, A certain man went down from Jerusalem to Jericho, and fell among thieves, which stripped him of his raiment, and wounded him, and departed, leaving him half dead. And by chance there came down a certain priest that way: and when he saw him, he passed by on the other side. And likewise a Levite, when he was at the place, came and looked on him, and

passed by on the other side. But a certain Samaritan, as he journeyed, came where he was: and when he saw him, he had compassion on him, And went to him, and bound up his wounds, pouring in oil and wine, and set him on his own beast, and brought him to an inn, and took care of him. And on the morrow when he departed, he took out two pence, and gave them to the host, and said unto him, Take care of him; and whatsoever thou spendest more, when I come again, I will repay thee. Which now of these three, thinkest thou, was neighbour unto him that fell among the thieves? And he said, He that shewed mercy on him. Then said Jesus unto him, Go, and do thou likewise.

—Luke 10:30-37, KJV

It's one of the most familiar parables of Jesus. As a little background, the Samaritans were hated by the Jews. The Samaritans were a mixed race that believed Samaria, not Jerusalem, was the place to worship God. The hatred toward them went back centuries. In the parable, Jesus describes the event of a man going down to Jerusalem falling among thieves who robbed him and left him for dead. By chance, along comes a priest who surveys the situation and passes by on the other side. Doing good can even be hard for someone who calls himself a man of God.

When I read this, I always wonder whether the priest was coming from or going to the temple. Often for many their Christianity starts and stops at the door of the church. It's no wonder the world looks at the church with a jaundiced eye. Especially when the world may be familiar with the teachings of Jesus but don't see it acted out in a practical way by those who call themselves believers.

Next comes a Levite. Not quite as high in the pecking order as a priest, but someone involved in the work of the Lord. The Levite tribe did not receive an inheritance of the land as the other tribes of Israel, their inheritance was the Lord himself. No small blessing, but with it came responsibilities that only they were permitted to do. The scriptures state, "when he was at the place, came and looked on him, and passed by on the other side" (Luke 10:32, KJV). I believe unlike the priest, the Levite got closer and more personal with the situation. He might have said, "This fellow looks in bad shape, let's see how bad he is. Half dead is pretty bad ... and for me to help this man out, it is going to take more than a nominal involvement. It's going to take time and I am supposed to be in church, the brothers are depending on me. Besides that, there's a chance I would be considered unclean if he up and dies on me." So, like the priest, whether going or coming from church, he passes by on the other side.

The other side speaks volumes to me of the point Jesus was making. To do good is hard there's no doubt about it. So rather than deal with the feelings of conviction, we willfully ignore the situation and get as far away from it as possible ... we pass on the other side. We close our eyes and ears to needs that are all around us, hoping someone else will help. It's easy to fault the priest and the Levite, but if we're honest with ourselves, we've all at times passed by on the other side avoiding getting our hands dirty. Jesus is concerned with what's going on inside us because He knows it will eventually be revealed in our actions. I believe God would rather us be honest with Him and say, "I see the needs but I made the decision to ‹pass on the other side' because doing good in this situation is hard and I won't do it." This gives God something to work with: an honest heart.

CHAPTER 3

Fear of Man

When I first came to know the Lord as a teenager, I was over-sensitive to maintaining good testimony. An example that comes to mind is my dad. He was an unbeliever and, at the time, was pretty much housebound suffering from Multiple Sclerosis. He would ask me to go to the local market to get him cigarettes and his favorite chewing tobacco. Sometimes I refused. I was paranoid that someone from the church would see me purchasing these tools of Satan. Though I don't recommend cigarettes, tobacco, or alcohol, the scriptures are clear: what comes out of your mouth is more important than what goes in. Being young and dumb in the faith, I very much had a pharisaical attitude. I would quote scriptures to my parents that didn't minister life but condemnation.

Looking back I realize I, for one, majored in minor things and minored in major ones. The Bible makes it clear the Kingdom of God is not meat and drink (external things) but righteousness, peace, and joy in the Holy Spirit (internal).

> For the kingdom of God is not meat and drink;
> but righteousness, and peace, and joy in the Holy
> Ghost.
>
> —Romans 14:17, KJV

awful thing; it can paralyze us from making rational de-
cisions. The world claims living by faith is irrational. I say, if we're living in fear that's irrational we will miss out on God's best for us. There are 365 "fear nots" in the Bible, I guess for every day of the year. If something is mentioned that often in the Word, it should make us take pause.

It's a battle all of us face. It's one that I had to overcome in many areas of my life. After coming to know Jesus, I felt a call to minister His Word. For someone who had many insecurities, including speaking in front of people, this was definitely a stretch. If I had to give an oral book report in front of the class, I was pet-rified. I would always volunteer to go first to get it out of the way because the pressure of fear was numbing. When I turned my life over to Christ, this fear didn't leave automatically; it was a giant I had to face.

In 1971, a pastor friend of mine, Henry Howells, told me about Christ For the Nations Institute (CFNI) founded by Gordon Lind-say, located in Dallas, Texas. I was a senior in high school and was accepted to Penn State, but was directed by the Lord to head to the Lone Star State instead. Unfortunately, I had no money to attend a Bible School. I made the commitment in my heart I was going to go if I needed to hitchhike there. I figured if God leads, He will meet the need.

Two months prior to the start of school, a job opened up as a brick layer helper for my uncle. This provided me enough mon-ey for the first two months of rent and tuition, and money to fly down. The third day I was there I mentioned to a lady, who helped with the housing, my need for a job. She told me Piggly Wiggly was hiring and pointed me in the direction of the store. Not know-ing anything about the area, I got turned around and headed in a different direction where I came across a Piggly Wiggly. I stopped in and told them I was looking for a job. It just so happened Piggly Wiggly's regional manager was there and hired me on the spot. The job allowed me to go to classes in the morning and work in the evening. God used Piggly Wiggly to help pay my way through school. What's interesting is when I went back to the lady who told me about Piggly Wiggly, she said I went to the wrong store. I thought at the time I actually went to the right store.

———————

At Bible school, we had a daily morning Chapel. One of our assignments was to conduct one of those services including preaching. Imagine a fellow who is afraid to be before people required to preach to a group of soon-to-be ministers.

On an interesting note, I had the privilege of being in the same class as two well-known names in Christian ranks, Benson Idahosa from Nigeria, and the highly-talented gospel singer Russ Taff.

Referred to as the father of Pentecostalism in Nigeria, Benson Idahosa was the founder of Church of God Mission International and Benson Idahosa University in Benin City, Nigeria. His impact on the continent of Africa can still be felt today.

Russ Taff is the winner of six Grammy Awards and eighteen Gospel Music Dove Awards. Russ was also a former member of the Imperials. His inspiring life journey was featured in the movie, *Russ Taff: I Still Believe.*

Joyce Meyer has a saying I love. She says, "Do it afraid." That was me. I lined up Joe Paris, also a fellow student, to play the accordion (kind of unusual, but why not?) and lead worship, then I would preach. Do you know the subject I chose for my first sermon? Fear. I can't recall exactly what I said or the scriptures I used, but I do remember the response. I received a standing ovation from my classmates. I think they sensed how much of a battle it was for me to speak and wanted to encourage me in the fight. I've been preaching ever since. We need to be encouragers.

───────

Here's a wild story concerning Bible school and how God orders our steps. After attending CFNI in the early seventies, I didn't return to the Dallas, Texas school for a visit for more than forty years. Having had some correspondence with the school, my wife and I decided to visit. When I made that decision to fly to Texas, a tremendous battle of fear gripped my heart. I felt I should go, but fear once again raised its ugly head. What's strange, I had at that time flown numerous times, including trips to Latin America and Europe. I believe through the prayers of my wife and a good friend Scott Hinkle, who was a classmate at CFNI, we made the trip.

A side note on Scott: many traveling preachers call themselves evangelists but are really only preachers without a church. I believe Scott is a modern-day evangelist with a burden for souls. He's led numerous evangelistic trips to Mardi Gras. He has taught on soul-winning to churches and schools throughout the world for more than half a century. He and his wife, Nancy, truly have a heart to reach the lost.

When my wife and I arrived at the school, we were kindly greeted by the late John Hollar, a director and teacher, who took us on a tour of the campus. It sure had changed and grown over the years. It was an on-going testimony of God's faithfulness. As I shared with John how I came to know Jesus and ended up at CFNI, he asked me to speak to his class the next day on the Holy Spirit. He said there would be about 400 students in the class from all over the world. I was a no-name and John didn't really know me, so speaking to his class was totally unexpected; we came only to tour the campus. I spoke and we had a tremendous move of the

Spirit with many students being touched and baptized in the Holy Spirit.

When I returned home, I was praying one morning and the Lord reminded me of a personal prophecy that was spoken over me at a minister's conference in Canada. I've never guided my life by personal prophecies, but was always leery of them, maybe because of abuses I've seen over the years.

The conference provided a cassette recording of the prophecy, which I threw in my sock drawer after the conference. I couldn't even remember what was on it, absolutely no clue at all.

I took the cassette to the office to play on a cassette player I had stored in the attic. Our family had made the move to CD's so I didn't even have a cassette player at home. I played it and broke down in tears. Here's an excerpt from the prophecy from someone I never met and who knew nothing of my background.

> I saw a herd of sheep, sheep rather than being white were all different colors. There were black ones, yellow ones, blue ones all different colors and I thought this is a very strange-looking picture with sheep with so many different colors and you were walking alongside them they were following then I understood what they were. They were nations, people from all different nations, and they were all gathered together and you were putting feed down on the ground for them and they were running to eat that feed, the feed was the Word of God. I believe the Holy Spirit is going to expand in this area, there will be many nations, many different types of people from all

over the world that you are going to minister to. They are all going to be in one place. Whether it's going to be a church, a building, I have no idea. But there is a large number of them from all different nations.

She used the word "nations" six times in the prophecy and never used "country". I was speaking at Christ for the *Nations*. What was equally amazing is the prophecy was given to me exactly twelve years to the month, almost to the day, prior to going to CFNI to simply visit the campus. The devil tried to stop me from "doing good" by teaching the class. I'm reminded you can't connect the dots going forward, only looking back.

Now we see things imperfectly, like puzzling reflections in a mirror, but then we will see everything with perfect clarity. All that I know now is partial and incomplete, but then I will know everything completely, just as God now knows me completely.

—I Corinthians 13:12, NLT

CHAPTER 4

Doing Good Intentionally

Acts of kindness need to be intentional. We can't leave them to chance. What do I mean by this? We do things to get a result. We intentionally go to work to get a paycheck. We take vitamins to stay healthy. We raise our children to the best of our ability so when they are older, they are productive citizens and successful. We wouldn't dream about leaving these things to chance. We plan our lives around intentional acts. In the same way, doing good needs to be a way of life.

It's early spring. I'm planning on planting a garden this year. I already spoke with my neighbor about him tilling the ground (good neighbors are good). As soon as the garden is tilled, I'll head to the local garden center to pick out my favorite vegetables to plant.

It's not enough though to have a garden tilled, smooth out the ground, and go purchase the plants. I need to get them *into* the ground. Unless I intentionally dig the holes, plant and water the vegetables, I will never enjoy the fruit of my labor.

I need to "do it". It may take thought, planning, and cooperation, but the critical part is *doing* it. Often this is where we fail as individuals and as a church.

The paralysis of analysis can cripple us in doing good. Jesus said simply don't let your left hand know what your right hand doeth; don't get caught up in the analysis but simply make it happen just go ahead and do it in secret.

But when thou doest alms, let not thy left hand know what thy right hand doeth.

—Matthew 6:3, KJV

The fifth book in the New Testament is commonly known as "Acts" but it's actually the "Acts of the Apostles." I'm afraid today if it was written for the modern church, it would be the "Analysis of the Apostles."

The Word is clear on the fact the doers of the Word are justified, not those who merely hear the Word. I want to deal with how to "do the do." I preached a sermon several years ago referring to a television commercial promoting Mountain Dew®. The theme of the commercial was to "Do the Dew." Get everything out of your life by drinking this soft drink. It may be a stretch when it comes to guzzling sugar water, but the only way we're going to really enjoy this Christian life is by "doing the do." It's not just learning more scripture verses and showing up to church on Sunday, but putting into practice what the Word says.

———

Jesus illustrates this in the parable of two men: one who built his house on the sand; the other on a rock.

> And why call ye me, Lord, Lord, and do not the things which I say? Whosoever cometh to me, and heareth my sayings, and doeth them, I will shew you to whom he is like: He is like a man which built an house, and digged deep, and laid the foundation on a rock: and when the flood arose, the stream beat vehemently upon that house, and could not shake it: for it was founded upon a

rock. But he that heareth, and doeth not, is like a man that without a foundation built an house upon the earth; against which the stream did beat vehemently, and immediately it fell; and the ruin of that house was great.

—Luke 6:46-49, KJV

The storm came to both men's lives, the person whose house withstood the storm was a doer and not just a hearer.

In the scripture, it says the man who built his house on the rock "dug deep." It takes effort to build upon the rock of God's Word. Digging a ditch by hand is hard work, at times serving God is as well. It takes time and commitment. You may even get a few "calluses" on your hands. But just like building a house, the foundation, though not seen, is vital to a successful build. A casual approach to the things of God and His Word, which is so prevalent today. I'm sorry to say it won't hold up when the storms of life hit. Many have left the church because the "Gospel" they were taught never required anything from them but to come to church on Sunday and throw a couple bucks in the offering. When the storm hits, and no one is exempt from storms, they couldn't understand why what they believed was shaken. Unfortunately, they didn't dig deep to let the Word become a reality in their everyday lives. Jesus also illustrated this at the last supper.

Ye call me Master and Lord: and ye say well; for so I am. If I then, your Lord and Master, have washed your feet; ye also ought to wash one another's feet. For I have given you an example, that ye should do as I have done to you. Verily, verily, I say unto you, The servant is not greater than his lord; neither he that is sent greater than he that sent him. If ye know these things, happy are ye if ye do them.

—John 13:13-17, KJV

Jesus, the Master and Lord, washes the disciples' feet, giving us an example of how we should serve others in humanity.

In verse seventeen, Jesus sums up what "doing the do" is. "If ye know these things, happy are ye if ye do them."

There are a lot of unhappy Christians because they have never gone beyond the "knowing" to enter in the "doing."

Three Heart Attitudes Needed to "Do the Do"

A WANT TO

God never forces us to do anything. He has given us a free will to make decisions whether right or wrong. He won't force us to act on His Word. If we're hindered by thinking we're not qualified, gifted, or talented enough, let me tell you: availability is more important to God than ability. Having a "want to" gives God something to work with.

HUMILITY

But he giveth more grace. Wherefore he saith, God resisteth the proud, but giveth grace unto the humble.

—James 4:6, KJV

No one has all the answers and no one can do everything, but God can give us the grace to do the do. According to the Mariam-Webster Dictionary, one of the definitions of grace is, "unmerited divine assistance given to humans for their regeneration or sanctification." If we need grace, and we all do, it's there to do the do.

PLIABILITY

We need to guard our hearts so they don't become hardened by exposure to the world. It's like Play-Doh left out of its airtight container: no matter how pliable and colorful the modeling clay once was, the air will harden it.

> Take heed, brethren, lest there be in any of you an evil heart of unbelief, in departing from the living God. But exhort one another daily, while it is called To day; lest any of you be hardened through the deceitfulness of sin. For we are made partakers of Christ, if we hold the beginning of our confidence steadfast unto the end;
>
> —Hebrews 3:12-14, KJV

The deceitfulness of sin can rob us if we're not always on guard. We need to be pliable in God's hand, He's the potter, we're the clay. Let Him fashion us as an instrument to do the do.

Ways to Intentionally Move into *Doing* Good

PRAY

We all know we should do it, but do we?

I distinctly remember an admonition from one of our Bible School teachers at the end of the school year. Make sure you pray, if only for five or ten minutes a day, make it a habit. I kind of scoffed at that in my mind. Being in the Bible School cocoon, ten minutes a day of prayer was like falling off a log. Boy did I get humbled when I went out in the real world with all the daily pressures vying for my time. You have to make prayer a priority. Quality is more important than quantity. So set a time (mornings are good). If you're not praying now, try it for five minutes. If you pray for five minutes, do it ten. Consistency brings more results than one all-night prayer meeting every three years. Pray for your family, pray for your neighbors, pray for brothers and sisters, pray for guidance in your life, pray for the lost, pray for the leaders.

I've made a habit of praying for eight guys. I write down their names at the beginning of the year. and try to pray for them daily. I picked it up from a well-known teacher and instituted it in my life which has yielded results.

Don't say prayers, but talk with God as if he's right there with you—because He is. Prayers shouldn't be a one-way conversation, be still and let Him speak to your heart.

BE A WITNESS

Many of us have difficulty sharing our faith because we're intimidated not only by others but by our lack of confidence in the area. How about starting by leaving a tract somewhere if you're that scared? Let it slip out of your pocket so no one sees you leave it. Mention in conversation with an unsaved how God has blessed you in a certain way. Share your testimony when an opportunity lends itself. We think witnessing is standing on the street corner and preaching at ears going by. God can use that, but the most successful soul-winning efforts are with people we have a relationship with.

Start simple and let your doing increase.

LOVE YOUR NEIGHBOR

Do something kind. Cut their grass or leave a pie on their front porch with a little note and tell them you appreciate them being your neighbor. Loving your neighbor needs to start somewhere, let it start with a simple act of kindness. This is the "doing of the Word." Maybe you don't get along with your neighbor, all the more reason to, by faith, do something that will surprise them and you at the same time. God can use it to mend fences. Always take the high road and be quick to forgive.

GIVE

The Word is clear about our responsibility to be givers. If you don't see that, or are not convinced, look in your Bible concordance about giving. You'll see Jesus talked more about money than heaven or hell.

Stretch your giving by faith from where you now are to give more. If you're not a tither, you should be. But if you feel your faith isn't that strong, work toward it. Increase from where you're at and by faith systemically, build your giving to the tithe and beyond. You've heard the saying, "you can't out-give God". It's true. I've experienced it in my own life

LABOR IN THE AREA THAT YOU ARE GIFTED OR YOU FEEL GOD IS CALLING YOU TO DO

How do you do this? For instance, if you feel God has called you to be a teacher of His Word, then you should be a student of the Word. Look for simple opportunities to develop your calling.

I believe the church has failed by not properly training those whom God has called. For instance, we stick well-meaning people in a children's church class to teach without any instruction and hope it works out. It's not fair to them or to the people they are trying to instruct.

Whatever God has placed in your heart, take steps to do it. Don't wait for lightning to strike you or a vision from heaven. Move out in faith. The Jordan River didn't part until the priests carrying the Ark of the Covenant stepped in the water. Step out by faith and watch God work.

Kenneth H. McGaffic

CHAPTER 5

Compound Interest

At the end of every year, I begin planning for the new year. Though I enjoy the holidays, I'm more comfortable in the daily routines of life and setting goals once I get through the holidays. I buy my new daily planner (I'm old school). I still write down my appointments as I've done for the last twenty-five years. I have a stack of planners to prove it. I prayerfully consider eight men I feel God wants me to pray for daily throughout the year, and I also make decisions concerning our finances.

One of the decisions I recently made was this: Linda, my wife of forty-plus years, and I would cash in some United States savings bonds that reached maturity and were no longer earning interest. These are bonds we've had for more than thirty years. I still remember why I started purchasing them.

We were married for about ten years and had limited income. When I say limited, I mean at times we had to cash in the pop bottles to make ends meet. (Don't know what that means? Ask your grandparents.) We would also eat popcorn and drink water so it would swell up our stomachs (maybe it wasn't that bad). I knew I had to take steps to secure my family's long-term financial future for college, retirement, and such. I also knew if I put the money in a passbook savings account, at the first need, whether imagined or real, I would quickly pull the money out and spend it (no one knows you better than yourself). So, I decided buying savings bonds was my best bet if I was really serious about saving for the future.

So at the beginning of the year, I went online to see the values of these savings bonds today. I was amazed at how they had grown. I always understood the benefit of compound interest, but to see it work on our behalf in such a dramatic way simply amazed me. I told my wife if I would have known how much they could increase in value, I would have bought savings bonds at higher denominations. We laughed because we knew at that time we used what little extra money we had to buy them. This brings me to the point of where do we go from here?

I believe we need to start doing good with what God has placed in our trust. Many a sermon has been preached on the three T's: time, talent, and treasure.

The points are worth repeating. In reality, we don't own anything, we are simply stewards (managers) of what God has entrusted to us. When we pass from this life, we take nothing with us. I've never seen a hearse with a U-Haul trailer pulled behind it. An illustration I enjoy is "living life is like playing the game Monopoly, when the game is over, everything goes back in the box" (James Dobson, Focus on the Family). Many a well-known ministry has gone downhill because the pastor, or person in charge, thought they owned what God had entrusted to them and not that they were simply stewards (managers). They put unqualified family members in positions of authority and the ministry suffered. They want to continue their family's "legacy" at the expense of what's best for God's work. It's actually selfishness.

Let me illustrate it this way. If my friend lends me his truck, I'll be more careful with his truck than if it was my truck. I'll make sure I don't scratch it, it's clean and filled up with gas when I return it to him. It's his truck, he put it in my care, he entrusted it to me. I'll do everything in my power to not abuse that trust. Get the point?

We need to be intentional with the use of our time, talent, and treasure. "Our" is the key word here. Our responsibility lies with what God has entrusted to us, not the time, talent, or treasure of our neighbor. We need to keep our eye on our ball. I had the privilege of coaching both of my girls in softball. I'm not sure how good of a coach I was, but I enjoyed being with my daughters and our teams ended up being competitive. As a coach, one aspect of hitting I emphasized was to keep your eye on the ball, watch the ball, hit the ball. Don't worry about what your teammates are doing in the dugout, what the opposing team is saying, or that your boyfriend is in the stands. When you're at bat keep your eye on the ball. We often are unsuccessful because we lose focus on the task at hand; what God has given us to manage. We start comparing ourselves with others, coveting the 3T's of someone else, rather than keeping our eye on our ball.

One of my favorite stories in the New Testament is found in the last chapter of John.

> Verily, verily, I say unto thee, When thou wast young, thou girdest thyself, and walkedst whither thou wouldest: but when thou shalt be old, thou shalt stretch forth thy hands, and another shall gird thee, and carry thee whither thou wouldest not. This spake he, signifying by what death he should glorify God. And when he had spoken this, he saith unto him, Follow me. Then Peter, turning about, seeth the disciple whom Jesus loved following; which also leaned on his breast at supper, and said, Lord, which is he that betrayeth thee? Peter seeing him saith to Jesus, Lord, and

what shall this man do? Jesus saith unto him, If I
will that he tarry till I come, what is that to thee?
follow thou me.

—John 21:18-22, KJV

Jesus is resurrected from the dead and speaking to Peter about
what Peter's future would be and how he would eventually die.
Peter looks over at John and says, "How about him?" Imagine this,
after three years of intense training by Jesus himself, seeing miracles
and the resurrection of Christ, Peter took his eye off the ball and
was worried about John. So, don't get discouraged, there is hope
for us.

Jesus redirected Peter's focus and said, "what is that to thee?
follow thou me" (John 21:22, KJV).

We each have a different course to run in life, it's important for us
to heed the admonition, "hoe in our own row." We have enough
to keep us busy on our course rather than getting caught in being
God's umpire on what is happening in other's lives.

Use your gifting, your natural abilities, internal leanings, the
things you love to do to serve God and run the race. Your ultimate
goal in this Christian life is not "full-time" ministry. You're already
a full-time minister if you're a Christian. You need to serve God
where you're planted and not let Satan (the accuser of the brethren)
bring discouragement in your life by having you compare yourself
to others. Paul, the apostle, wrote in a letter to Timothy, "I have
fought a good fight, I have finished my course, I have kept the
faith" (2 Timothy 4:7, KJV). Paul finished his course, not Peter's,
James', or John's. He kept his eye on the ball and in turn God
granted him the privilege to write most of the New Testament.

To sum it up, following Jesus means being concerned about our individual work with Him and the 3T's we've been blessed to manage.

One of the best pieces of advice anyone ever shared with me as a young believer was to "keep my eyes on Jesus."

> [looking away from all that will distract us and] focusing our eyes on Jesus, who is the Author and Perfecter of faith [the first incentive for our belief and the One who brings our faith to maturity], who for the joy [of accomplishing the goal] set before Him endured the cross, disregarding the shame, and sat down at the right hand of the throne of God [revealing His deity, His authority, and the completion of His work].
>
> —Hebrews 12:2, AMP

It's a simple statement, but it has deep truth. It doesn't take too long after you begin your walk with Christ, that you realize Christians are still people with many of the same hang-ups as unbelievers.

My eyes were opened when I was new in the faith. I saw how some Christians spoke negatively about fellow believers. I thought to myself, *This shouldn't be this way. This is no different than the people out in the world.* I ended up avoiding certain people in the church because the ones they were talking about were very close to me. To be honest, except for the grace of God, this would have destroyed my faith.

I've also witnessed first-hand when someone leaves a fellowship or group of believers for any reason, they often become an open target for criticism. It's almost like they were great when they were part of our "team," but now since they are gone, they're no good. As one bumper sticker read, "Christians aren't perfect, just forgiven."

If you have your eyes on others, on circumstances, or even yourself (yes you have hang-ups too), you'll strike out on being a good steward. Keep your eyes on Jesus, He'll never fail you.

CHAPTER 6

Use What You Have

God spoke to Moses from the burning bush and called him to deliver the Israelites from Egypt. Moses questioned God and how He would make that happen. God simply asked him, "What is in your hand?"

> And Moses answered and said, But, behold, they will not believe me, nor hearken unto my voice: for they will say, The Lord hath not appeared unto thee. And the Lord said unto him, What is that in thine hand? And he said, A rod.
>
> —Exodus 4:1-2, KJV

We need to use what is entrusted to us today and let him multiply its effectiveness for His kingdom, even though what we have may seem insignificantly small to us.

The Bible is filled with stories of God using insignificant people and things for His glory. For Moses, it was a rod to deliver Israel from Egyptian bondage (Exodus 4:1-4). For David, it was a sling to defeat the giant Goliath (1 Samuel 17:40). A net in Peter's hand hauled in a great catch of fish. Even though Peter's initial thought was, *We toiled all night and caught nothing.* (Luke 5:1-11). Jesus fed more than 5,000 people with a young lad's lunch (John 6:1-13).

Samson defeated the Philistines with the jawbone of an ass (Judge 15:15). A handful of flour and a little oil sustained a widow and her son during a drought when she was obedient to the prophet Elijah (1 Kings 17:9-16).

These are just a few Bible examples. And how about this one?

Jesus was near the temple treasury one day with His disciples watching the people dropping in their offerings. He told his disciples that a poor widow woman gave more than the very rich even though she only gave a couple pennies compared to their large amounts. He said she gave all she had (Mark 12:41-44). We need to give all in doing good though it may seem small. Begin where you are, do what you can, and leave the final results to the Lord.

For example, it would be wonderful if all of us could move to a far off land to run an orphanage. Or maybe to go into the mission field to bring the Gospel to some remote tribe. But just as the widow gave what she had, God hasn't gifted all of us with that calling. By giving to support a child in a third world country, supporting Bible translators, or going on a short-term mission trip God can multiply what we have done in faith. We'll be surprised at the rewards on that final day. Just as I was surprised to see the value of just how much the savings bonds grew. In fact, Albert Einstein said, "Compound interest is the eighth wonder of the world. He who understands it, earns it. He who doesn't, pays it." Who am I to question old Albert?

Ecclesiastes 12:1 tells us to, "remember now thy Creator in the days of thy youth" (KJV). Coming to know Jesus at an early age can save us from many (not all) heartaches living in this fallen world. The enemy is always there to throw us curve balls. We're not exempt from these trials simply because we name the name of Christ. But what I've come to appreciate is that when a young person comes to know Christ, he has the benefit of seeing his "doing good" compound over many years. Obviously, we're not saved by "doing good" for then Jesus wouldn't have had to die for our sins.

But what I'm saying is what a privilege we have to invest into doing good over many years. Just as I was surprised at the compound results of the little amount socked away, those little ways of doing good I believe will increase exponentially, and only in eternity will we be able to realize the full impact of our doing good!

———————

I recently read an article about a fellow who was hired several years ago to sell advertising for a local newspaper. Oddly, the manager who hired him gave him some unusual hours to work. He had him come in after all the other salespeople were gone on the road. Why did the manager do that? He didn't want the negativity and sour attitudes toward certain businesses to hinder the new hire from going out and selling. The new salesperson knew no history of why they wouldn't buy; he just went and sold. His enthusiasm for the job sold accounts that had never bought before. The manager was smart enough to know this man's fellow workers would show him the paralysis of analysis. After a while, this fellow became the supervisor of some of these same people before moving on to more lucrative opportunities. He didn't see the obstacles, he saw only the opportunities. He didn't have someone telling him why he couldn't; he just did it.

When the children of Israel came out of Egypt they were promised a land flowing with milk and honey. There was only one obstacle—no not the giants, though the giants were there. No, it was their inability to see that God's promises were greater than the obstacles they faced. The giants were big in their sight, but even more telling, they viewed themselves as grasshoppers. Not a very glamorous self-image.

To do good we need to look past our own insufficiencies and perceived obstacles and just do it. We need to do good, regardless of whether we're afraid or whether everyone is on board with us.

I've found if you feel God has called you to do something, enter into the task as if you will be doing it by yourself. Because often you will be. Your vision is not everyone's vision. Whether our own lack of confidence shouts you'll fail, everyone is going to laugh, or you're not worthy, just do it and you'll find amazingly enough, God will show up and help you through the process. The Bible says we are co-laborers with God.

> For we are labourers together with God: ye are
> God's husbandry, ye are God's building.
>
> —1 Corinthians 3:9, KJV

God is right there with us as we do good. Doing good is labor. Pleasant thoughts and analysis is not where God shows himself strong on our behalf. God is a present help as we enter the promised land in faith by doing.

CHAPTER 7

Doing Good Does Not Always Work Out as Planned

O ur church purchased a farm on the highest spot in our county where they hoped to place a transmitting tower that would be used for television and radio ministry. This was before the explosion of Christian television we see today. One of the pastors' mothers lived on the farm. Her grandson and I would visit her often. She had mentioned to me she would love to have the garage door blocked up rather than being open. Being enclosed would work better for storage. Having had time on my hands, being single, and having worked a couple summers with my uncle as a bricklayer's helper, I said to myself, *How hard would it be to block up the opening?* I bought everything I needed to do the job. This was on me; I wanted to "do good." With great enthusiasm, I started early one morning to tackle this job. I thought it was going to be a piece of cake … I assumed.

It didn't take me long to discover my enthusiasm to "do good" didn't offset my lack of ability. After laying a few rows of block, I couldn't match up the mortar joints with block that was already there. It looked like a mess and I didn't know how to make it right. I was too far into it to start over. The pastor, whose mother I was trying to be a blessing to, eventually came out and fixed my mistake with a two-inch mortar joint.

Since then, after many futile attempts to use my limited construction ability, I've settled on the fact that, for me, paying someone to do construction projects puts me way ahead in the long run. (My wife reminds me how the same pastor lovingly mentioned from the pulpit how I was great at tearing things up when our church was looking for volunteers to do some demolition work for a church project.)

Sometimes "doing good" doesn't give us the desired results. But if our hearts are in the right place and looking to "do good," God will bring opportunities our way that will match our ability to meet the need.

CHAPTER 8

Doing Good Impacts People

Several years ago my wife and I visited some friends who were missionaries in Central America. We had been on various short-term mission trips over the years, so the living conditions of some of the locals didn't surprise us.

What did catch our attention though was a family that our friends introduced us to who had tuberculosis and were in noticeably bad health. I asked our friends about their condition and they told us they were sick from sleeping on the ground.

My wife and I decided right then and there we wanted to "do good" by providing them mattresses (more like sleeping mats). This is something we were able to provide through the finances God had blessed us with. Later that year our missionary friends sent us photos of mattresses we had purchased (a lot of mattresses) that filled their truck and house which God, through us, provided. Since then we've been able to "do good" in the way of buying beds and mattresses for ministries in several countries throughout the world. We feel it's a practical way to show God's love and help spread the Gospel. We responded to God's leading and used what was in our hands.

Linda previously worked for a large corporation that matched her charitable gifts to non-profits if they were in the United States. We took advantage of it and saw our gifting double in supporting Christian ministries. I'm not sure if the corporate foundation had that in mind when they set up the program, but we didn't care, we jumped on it to "do good." Why not?

"Doing good does us good" Arthur P. Ciaramicoli wrote in *The Stress Solution*. Maybe that's what Jesus meant when He said, "It's more blessed to give than to receive"

> I have shewed you all things, how that so labouring ye ought to support the weak, and to remember the words of the Lord Jesus, how he said, It is more blessed to give than to receive.
>
> —Acts 20:35, KJV

Early in our marriage, we decided to take in foster children. My wife was a foster child herself, so she had a burden for them. I'll never forget our first child. It was a real eye-opener on how it's not always easy to do good. My wife was expecting an innocent little seven-year-old boy to come walking through the door. But she was in for a surprise when the first words that came out of his mouth were, "My favorite group is KISS." And, "Where's the toy box for my toys?" She called me and said, "Butch, you need to come home."

Little did we know "Billy" had been in eight different foster homes at the tender age of seven. He was already hardened to the foster care system and figured if this didn't work out, they would ship him to live with someone else. It was heartbreaking as I look back, but we were determined to do good. We would get so many notes from his teacher about his bad conduct. She decided instead to send us a note when he was good. He wanted so much to go live with his mother but she had her own problems and couldn't take care of him. He would ask me who his dad was. Unfortunately, I had no idea.

I sat him down one day and said, "Billy, you can act as bad as you want, but you're staying here until you go back and live with your mom. You're not going to a different foster home." We loved him, disciplined him, and provided for him as if he was our own son, knowing that one day he would leave. After a period of time, he was returned to his mother. Years later, he came and told us we had made an impact on his life. Doing good is not easy.

Another time we took in a brother and sister, a ten-month-old and three-year-old. Our oldest daughter was two at the time. Their mother was nowhere to be seen, and they were living with their father. Tragically, he raped and murdered a girl at the local supermarket and ended up on death row. It was a sad story. And it wasn't an easy time for us. We had limited income, and taking care of three kids that close in age was a challenge.

Linda and I joked years later how that in the wintertime, taking the children to church after getting them in their Sunday "go to meeting" clothes, snow suits, and in their car seats, you wondered why you even bothered. Before that time, I was critical of families who came late to church. No more. I saw how just getting to church was an act of faith. The brother and sister stayed with us for about a year before leaving to live with their mother.

We became foster parents of a fifteen-month-old boy who only weighed fifteen pounds. The police told us that when he was taken from the parents, the home was in the most deplorable condition he had ever witnessed, including dog feces all over the floor. Linda and I looked at each other when we heard that. We knew the father was a cook at a nationwide chain restaurant. The child had never eaten solid food and couldn't stand up. It was very time consuming just to try to get some nutrients in him. And being neglected the way he was affected him in other ways. My wife nursed him back to health, and he was eventually adopted by a loving couple.

The most difficult time of foster care was the time we were asked to take a baby girl right from the hospital where she was born. The child was born with a cleft lip and palate. If you've never dealt with a baby in that condition, it's hard to imagine the effort it takes just to feed them. I give my wife all the credit in the world. She's the type of person who flies under the radar to show love and kindness. We had the baby operated on in Children's Hospital in Pittsburgh, a wonderful facility, to repair the lip and palate. My wife slept on the floor beside the baby's bed for about four days during the baby's recovery. Linda had to learn how to properly feed and take care of the baby until the surgery healed up.

We never entered into foster care with the intention of adopting one of the children. That changed with this little one. We had her for about a year and a half. She had limited contact with the mother who could not take care of her. The child's uncle decided he wanted her after all this time. We took it to court believing it would be best for her to stay with us and lost. We might have thought differently, but her uncle had been with the child only twice over eighteen months. We had the hearing in the morning at 9:00 a.m. and once the verdict was given, we had to turn the child over to the uncle at 3:00 p.m. It was one of the hardest things we ever had to do.

It's hard to do good.

CHAPTER 9

Orphans from Guatemala

Throughout the years, Linda and I would go on short-term mission trips. We usually went at separate times so one of us could stay home with the kiddos. One of our first few trips was to Guatemala to do construction work on an orphanage that had about sixty children. The construction crew consisted of a group from Michigan and our group of believers from western Pennsylvania. The children of the orphanage were under the care of a lady known as Sister Charlotte. On one of my first trips there, we built a large dormitory with a water-cooling tank (the water was heated by a volcano, so it had to be cooled down). I look back still in wonderment of what our group did in only twelve days. It's amazing what can be accomplished when you have talented hardworking individuals with a mind to work.

Two of the orphan girls I met there had terrible back deformities that made them walk bent to one side. The orphanage did not have the money to help these girls even if the medical care was available in the country.

Sometime later, Linda and I were at a Shriner's Circus in Pittsburgh with our daughter, Erin. During the circus, the announcer was putting on a drive to recruit children who may need their services. The Shriner's Hospital treats children born with birth defects, or burn victims, etc. They do wonderful work at no charge to the patients. My wife looked at me and said, "Do you think they could help Miriam and Amalia, the two orphanage girls with back problems?" I wasn't sure, but I would find out.

One of my best friends, Sam, is a Shriner, and he put me in contact with Phil; he thought he could help. Phil said for us to send the X-rays to him and he would forward them to the decision-makers. Long story short, the Shriners decided they would try to help if we could get the girls to the states from Guatemala. Linda traveled to Guatemala, had Charlotte sign over the custody of the girls to her, and we flew them up to Pittsburgh. The girls had never been on a plane, and had never experienced many of the things we take for granted. Their only possessions in life were what they stored under their beds. We had to take both girls to the Shriner's Hospital in Chicago because their conditions were too bad for the Shriner's Hospital closest to us to help.

Shriner's ended up operating on Mariam who was suffering from scoliosis and curvature of the spine. Linda stayed in Chicago for most of that summer at the hospital. The operation saved Mariam's life because her condition was worsening and crushing her internal organs. It was a difficult and hard time before, during, and after the operation. Linda took the heat because Mariam at the time couldn't see that this was saving her life. She had to endure being in a halo to stretch her out, with steel rods placed in her back, and she wore a body cast for months. During that time, Miriam blamed Linda for the pain and everything she had to endure. Miriam stayed with us for about a year; it was a trying, but wonderful time.

A side note: Amalia was operated on a few years later and stayed with friends in Michigan. Both girls are doing great. I went on a teaching trip to Central America several years after they had been with us. Seeing the girls healthy and whole was beyond exciting.

Maybe you have made attempts to "do good" and were rejected for your efforts. Don't despair, you're in good company.

Moses was rejected at times by the same people he was leading out of bondage to a "good land."

David was rejected by Saul even though David only did him good.

Jesus himself, the Bible says, went about "doing good" healing the sick, raising the dead, freeing people from the grip of the devil, but was ultimately rejected by the people he came to help.

As I stated before, our motivation needs to please God. Because if we're looking for a pat on the back with the words "great job" from the ones we help, we may be waiting a good while.

CHAPTER 10

Receiving Good is Good

Over the years I've been on the receiving end of many "do good" acts by believers, as well as unbelievers. I could probably write a book on those alone, but there are a couple that stick out in my mind.

After graduating from Bible School I went home and got a job in a steel mill until I figured out what I was supposed to do with the rest of my life. Getting a job in a steel mill was pretty easy in the early seventies, especially in western PA where the mills were the only major employers. I was there for a couple of years but knew in my heart it wasn't my lifetime calling.

Our church at that time had a sister church in Detroit without a pastor who we supported by sending a team to minister there each weekend. I thought this might be an opportunity for me to get into "full-time" ministry. (Now I know as believers we are all in full-time ministry.) My pastor agreed it was worth exploring, so I went to my boss at the mill and told him my plans.

He told me rather than quitting, he wanted me to take a temporary leave for "continued education." This was highly unusual, but God gave me favor, so I agreed. I went and lived in the church for a short period, which included taking a bath in the baptismal (no showers), and helped in the ministry there. Though my intentions were right, I realized I wasn't prepared or ready to make a full-time commitment there.

God used the superintendent of the mill to "do good" on my behalf. I came home and took up where I left off at the mill with the same job and seniority I had in the past. I stayed there until I left to enter the occupation I'm still in today.

Another instance comes to mind when I was an associate pastor at a small church. I had cut back my schedule on my regular job so I could devote a couple days a week to the church. Finances were limited even though I received a small salary from the church and my wife worked. I had an old car that broke down and was on its last leg. I remember I was at home when my dad, who was an unbeliever at the time, came over and asked whether I was going to get my car fixed. Unfortunately, I could hardly afford to. He told me the "man upstairs wasn't going to help me," naturally referring to God. The very next day a couple from our church gave us an Oldsmobile Cutlass Supreme that was only a couple of years old and the church gave us $700 as well to fix anything that might be wrong with it.

A few days later I pulled up in front of my dad's home in my new car. I went in to tell him I wanted to show him something. He came out and asked where I got it, I simply said, "The man upstairs gave it to me." It's great to be on the receiving end of the "do goods" of other people.

As I was writing this book my daughter, Erin, posted online a "do good" act by Tanner, my eight-year-old grandson. She was taking Tanner and his older brother, Caleb, to school. They noticed a small blue bird whose feet were frozen to the ground in the snow. Tanner demanded his mother turn around so he could help this little bird.

He took his mom's hot coffee (it was a sacrifice for her) and melted the snow and ice around the bird's feet to free it. He then delicately placed it under a bush out of the weather. God was watching out for the bird through the eyes of my grandson. At a young age, he's already learned how to do good. I pray he'll never forget.

I have a neighbor named Bob. I believe every neighborhood would be better off with a Bob. He's the type of guy who, when it comes to remodeling, fixing a car, lawnmower, roof—you get it—he can do it or knows someone who can.

As I mentioned before, I'm not mechanically inclined and Bob knows it. I recently called him and said we need to get the snowblower we bought together tuned-up for a storm that was predicted. Even when I was saying "we" I actually meant "he" because I was of little use in tuning it up. He said he already had it ready.

One time I was assembling a power washer and couldn't get the nozzle end to attach. I gave Bob a call and related my dilemma and he said he would be right over. He came and flipped the end around and it snapped into place. I was trying to attach the wrong end. I felt stupid, but what I love about Bob is he never made me feel stupid. He knew who he was dealing with and simply went on his way. Doing good can be as simple as using our gifts in helping out a mechanically-challenged neighbor. It's just another aspect of doing good.

I've been blessed beyond measure by the family members, brothers and sisters in Christ, friends, and business associates that have enriched my life. Not to mention, the many ministers and teachers I have gleaned spiritual nourishment from their preaching and teaching.

I recently donated to a ministry of one of those teachers (internationally known). I kind of felt like (hope you don't mind the analogy) I had eaten at this minister's restaurant for many years, but let someone else pick up the bill. The donation was part of doing good. It wasn't a large contribution, but what's interesting is he called me to personally thank me for the support. (No, it wasn't one of those robocalls; I would have hung up.)

I related to him how I started following his ministry listening to reel-to-reel tapes (the precursor to cassette tapes) and how his teaching was such a blessing in my Christian journey. The simple phone call encouraged me, and I hope encouraged him as well.

Some people you know from far off, like this well-known minister, but others become part of your everyday life.

God smiled upon me when he brought two of those special friends into my life, Sam Ferguson and Rick Liptak. These friends blessed my wife and I over the years in so many ways more than can be written at this time, and truly exemplified people who do good.

Sam, by his own admission, is simply a farmer from a small town in Eastern Ohio. I was introduced to Sam by his cousin who I did advertising work for. Sam and I hit it off, and over the years, we became good friends and business associates. He was a mentor to me without him even knowing it. His wife Sue told me I was the son that Sam never had.

If I came home with a wild scheme or a way of getting out of something the wives wanted Sam and I to do, Linda would say, "You've been hanging around Sam again." Of course, I blamed it on Sam, that's what friends do.

Sam and I enjoyed many humorous experiences. One was when, as couples, we were promoters of a craft festival in Surry, VA, a community just across the James River from Williamsburg. When we first started the event, Sam offered to buy a couple of the workers breakfast from one of the vendors, thinking this was a one-shot deal. But do you know, the workers thought they got free breakfast for life? Each October when we held the event, they would thank Mr. Sam for the breakfast as they headed over to the vendor. Sam never told them otherwise. We just laughed and Sam paid. That's just a simple story of Sam's generosity.

I've seen Sam deal with difficult decisions in business, battling cancer, health issues in his family, and unexpected turns in life. When most would look for an easy way out, Sam would make the difficult decision to do good despite how it may affect him. I would question him about it, his response was always the same, "Kenny, that's what you do." His generosity and doing good is a way of life for Sam and has touched many.

I first got to really know Rick Liptak, or R.S. as he was called, on a construction mission trip to Guatemala. He was the only person I knew who could fall asleep as soon as his head hit the pillow. Not a minute later, not thirty seconds later, but instantly. He was an extraordinary storyteller. I always thought *if I could preach like he told stories, I would be the next Billy Graham.*

On one construction mission trip we went on, R.S.'s leg was bothering him which hindered him from going up and down on a ladder. I was up on a ladder trying to hang on while holding a board, hammer, and nail (you already know my gift is not building). Rick looked up and saw my dilemma. I can still hear him shout, "Boy, get down off that ladder!" I came down and he went up and finished the job.

R.S. was always there to help out anyone, or the church, in any way. Doing good can be hard, but he made it seem easier than what it was. He's gone on to be with the Lord now, but I've always thought (strange as it might be) that when I leave this life, R.S. will be there waiting for me at the gate of heaven to tell me stories of the other side.

CHAPTER 11

Do They Want Help?

In the scriptures, you'll find throughout Jesus' ministry of healing a very curious happening. Jesus would ask the person in distress what they wanted. Didn't Jesus, the Son of God, already know? It seems to me, the blind man wanted to see and the lame man desired to walk. Whether he needed them to make a statement of faith or to see if they actually wanted to be healed, I really don't know.

But sad to say, we can get comfortable in pretty much any situation if we're there long enough. You'll hear of women (or men) in abusive relationships that stay there even if they have a clear avenue out.

At times in doing good you'll find people not ready or willing to receive the good turn on their behalf. This can be very frustrating for a "do gooder." I use that term in the most respectful way.

Jesus is known as the Great Shepherd. As a shepherd, he leads his sheep he doesn't drive them. We cannot force a "do good" act on someone who is not open to receive it. No doubt we need to be intentional and look for opportunities "to do good to all men." But we need to be sensitive enough to know when to back off.

I know of ministers with a genuine love for people who overstep their bounds without even knowing it and get involved in something that is none of their business. Trying to do good, but not being sensitive to the one they were trying to minister to. The minister sees it as concern; they see it as intrusive.

What are some reasons why a person wouldn't be receptive of a "do good"? As I mentioned before, I'm not a psychologist but have a "been around the block" education as a pastor, business owner, husband, parent, child, friend, volunteer … you get the point, but these are some attitudes I've observed.

- Pride: *I can do it on my own. I don't need help from anybody, never have, never will.* You're delusional if that's your attitude. If it wasn't for those who've gone before, from parents to those who founded and protect our country, you wouldn't have any place to be a "cowboy".

- Low Self Esteem: *I'm not worthy to receive your help.* Who is? I guess this is a type of pride as well. Rather than having your nose in the air, you have it in the dirt. Look up and look for good. Humility is not thinking less of yourself; it's thinking of yourself less.

- Super Spiritual: *It's just me and Jesus. I would rather depend on God.* That's right, but believe it or not, He uses people. Who has God entrusted to spread the "good news"? Not angels—people.

- Others Need it More: If you look around the world and see all the desperate conditions people live in, if we're honest with ourselves, we have it pretty darn good. So it's really not a question of the level of need. A question for you, do we need to be at the lowest of low (and who would know that but God) before we can say no one needs it more than me?

If someone wants to do you good, be thankful and receive it gladly. I don't need dessert after the main course, but I sure enjoy it. Let me illustrate it.

My daughter, Kelly, and her husband recently visited me while I was in Florida. Unfortunately, my wife was stuck at home taking care of an ailing dog. Though my daughter and husband have a nice income, when they're with me, I like to pay when going out to eat (which we do a lot), golfing, to the movies, etc. Kelly in turn wants to "bless me" which I reluctantly accept. She tells me (both of my daughters are not wallflowers, they're not afraid of calling it what it is), "You need to be able to accept as well as give and not complain."

We were at a restaurant waiting in line to be seated, and I mentioned I like their coconut cake. After eating, I was too full for dessert. She didn't buy me a piece to go, she bought me a whole cake. She said that was the only way they sold it … I have my doubts. She wanted to "bless" her dad with a few extra pounds.

Did you ever consider that God is not stingy? In fact, He is extravagant in His dealing with mankind. Just look at creation. He didn't just create one kind of flower for us to enjoy, but thousands of them in all different colors. God placed billions and billions of stars in the sky, not for his enjoyment, but for ours.

Look how this is demonstrated in the life of Jesus.

The first miracle Jesus performed was turning water into wine. Not just any wine, but the best wine at the wedding.

> And saith unto him, Every man at the beginning
> doth set forth good wine; and when men have
> well drunk, then that which is worse: but thou
> hast kept the good wine until now.
>
> —John 2:10, KJV

Jesus told His disciples to cast their nets into the water one more time (even though they fished all night and caught nothing). When they pulled in the net, the fish that were caught almost sank the boat (that's extravagant).

> Now when he had left speaking, he said unto Simon, Launch out into the deep, and let down your nets for a draught. And Simon answering said unto him, Master, we have toiled all the night, and have taken nothing: nevertheless at thy word I will let down the net. And when they had this done, they inclosed a great multitude of fishes: and their net brake. And they beckoned unto their partners, which were in the other ship, that they should come and help them. And they came, and filled both the ships, so that they began to sink.
>
> —Luke 5:4-7, KJV

Jesus fed the 5,000. Everyone ate and was full, and there were twelve baskets left. (Jesus knows how to take care of his workers.)

> And when the day began to wear away, then came the twelve, and said unto him, Send the multitude away, that they may go into the towns and country round about, and lodge, and get victuals: for we are here in a desert place. But he said unto them, Give ye them to eat. And they said, We have no more but five loaves and two fishes; except we should go and buy meat for all this people. For they were about five thousand men. And he said to his disciples, Make them sit down by

fifties in a company. And they did so, and made them all sit down. Then he took the five loaves and the two fishes, and looking up to heaven, he blessed them, and brake, and gave to the disciples to set before the multitude. And they did eat, and were all filled: and there was taken up of fragments that remained to them twelve baskets.

—Luke 9:12-17, KJV

CHAPTER 12

What Else Does the Bible Say?

What else does the Bible say about doing good? Well, plenty. Look at these verses concerning Jesus.

> How God anointed Jesus of Nazareth with the Holy Ghost and with power; who went about doing good and healing all that were oppressed of the devil; for God was with him.
>
> —Acts 10:38, KJV

Jesus' life was exemplified in doing good, from healing the sick, to feeding the 5,000, casting out devils, blessing the children, teaching the principles of the kingdom, caring for the outcasts of the day, and ultimately laying down His life for you and me.

We, as Christians, which mean little Christs, should take the life of Jesus as an example to follow.

Jesus was anointed by God with the Holy Spirit to do good. Jesus said in John 5:30, "I can of my own self do nothing" (KJV). Jesus was dependent on the Holy Spirit to walk in obedience to the Father. The inter-workings of the Godhead, Father, Son, and Holy Spirit are difficult for our minds to wrap around. One thing I'm sure of, it was motivated by love and was demonstrated by doing good.

Let's look at some other "do good" scriptures:

Trust in the Lord, and do good; so shalt thou
dwell in the land, and verily thou shalt be fed.

—Psalm 37:3, KJV

Depart from evil, and do good; and dwell for
evermore.

—Psalm 37:27, KJV

But ye, brethren, be not weary in well doing.

—II Thessalonians 3:13, KJV

But to do good and to communicate forget not:
for with such sacrifices God is well pleased.

—Hebrews 13:16, KJV

These are only a few of the many verses that encourage us to do
good. Here is one that is a little harder to swallow.

But I say unto you which hear, Love your enemies, do good to them which hate you, Bless them
that curse you, and pray for them which despitefully use you. And unto him that smiteth thee
on the one cheek offer also the other; and him
that taketh away thy cloak forbid not to take thy
coat also. Give to every man that asketh of thee;
and of him that taketh away thy goods ask them
not again. And as ye would that men should do
to you, do ye also to them likewise. For if ye love
them which love you, what thank have ye? for sinners also love those that love them. And if ye do
good to them which do good to you, what thank

have ye? for sinners also do even the same. And if ye lend to them of whom ye hope to receive, what thank have ye? for sinners also lend to sinners, to receive as much again. But love ye your enemies, and do good, and lend, hoping for nothing again; and your reward shall be great, and ye shall be the children of the Highest: for he is kind unto the unthankful and to the evil. Be ye therefore merciful, as your Father also is merciful.

—Luke 6:27-36, KJV

The title of this book is, *It's Hard to Do Good*, and nothing illustrates it more than these scriptures from Jesus' Sermon on the Mount.

Jesus is exhorting us that to truly be the children of God we need to do more than just endure our enemies, but be proactive in doing good to them. It's sometimes hard enough doing good to those closest to us, but to those who hate you, those who despitefully use you, those who take advantage of you, those that rip you off? Jesus said to do them good.

In one town, after healing Peter's mother-in-law, it was said Jesus healed everyone that was brought to Him.

Now when the sun was setting, all they that had any sick with divers diseases brought them unto him; and he laid his hands on every one of them, and healed them.

—Luke 4:40, KJV

Jesus gave of his time to those who were thought to deserve it least: a Samaritan woman (John 4:5-26); the publicans and sinners (Matthew 11:15-19); Mary Magdalene who had seven devils cast out of her (Luke 8:1- 2); little children (Mark 10:13-16); and of course, twelve disciples who were uneducated, self-centered, and rough around the edges to say the least. Jesus even gave abundantly to Judas who would betray him.

And let's not forget the most well-known scripture which is held up at most every major sporting event and a famous football player put in his eye black: John 3:16, "For God so loved the world that He gave His only begotten Son, that whoever believes in Him should not perish but have everlasting life" (KJV).

God gave His best, His only begotten Son (talk about setting the example of doing good). Through that, anyone has an opportunity to find forgiveness of sins and come into a relationship with God.

CHAPTER 13

Doing Good to Those Who Take Advantage of the System

Taking advantage of the system, you know what that means, it can be a hard pill to swallow for those struggling to support their families and do good.

When we're in Florida, we attend a church that supports more than 200 missionaries monthly. It's not a megachurch, but they are a mission-minded, giving church sending support of at least $100 monthly to each missionary. I told my wife when we give to their mission fund it's like a missionary mutual fund touching lives all over the world. Giving is a great way to turn something temporal into something eternal.

This same church has a food bank where my wife and I volunteer. When volunteering, you really have to guard your heart when you see someone pull up in a vehicle nicer than yours, pop the trunk, and you see they've already hit the other food banks in the area. You say to yourself, *don't they know there are people in real need?* I know it's better for me to work in the back, packing grocery bags; I can keep a better attitude that way.

Or you're waiting in line at the grocery store and the person checks out in front of you, uses their public assistance card, and then buys a carton of cigarettes with cash.

The list goes on and on: people living together having kids without getting married so they can collect more welfare, or taking money under the table to stay on welfare and avoid paying taxes. If you're not careful you can become cynical, which can hinder you from doing good.

Here's where we need balance and discernment to know the difference.

When I served as associate pastor of a small church, we had a fellow who stopped by the church regularly for us to help him out with some money. This went on for a while. Then the pastor and I decided, *why not have him do some manual labor to earn the money rather than a handout?* He was a young guy in good health, so we thought it not unreasonable. He worked one time, took the money, and never came back. Who said doing good means free?

Jesus helped countless people but did not help everyone. There were many around the pool of Bethesda, but it recorded he only helped one lame man.

I think we do people a disservice by not having strings attached at times. God told Adam and Eve: by the sweat of your brow you'll eat your bread. Unfortunately, today many able-bodied people are eating, but not sweating. It's easy to get bullied into giving when our hearts are not in it. Don't you get tired of declining to give to their charity when you're checking out at the grocery store?

Just a word of caution: if you're going to err, err on the side of liberality. The Bible says, "the liberal soul shall be made fat."

> The liberal soul shall be made fat: and he that watereth shall be watered also himself.
>
> —Proverbs 11:25, KJV

When Jesus fed the 5,000, he didn't check their lunchbox to see if they were holding out; He just fed them.

Kenneth H. McGaffic

CHAPTER 14

Three Aspects of a Good Word

A good word can be a word of encouragement, instruction, or even comfort. I'm sure there are other aspects of a good word, but I would like to deal with these three.

Did you ever consider doing good can simply be saying a good word? The Bible states in Proverbs 25:11, "A word fitly spoken is like apples of gold in pictures of silver" (KJV).

A good word is something precious. A good word is not simply a thought; it needs to be spoken. It's like the old joke where a fellow is talking to his buddy and says, "I love my wife so much it takes everything in me not to tell her." He needed to tell her.

A Good Word of Encouragement

Walking this Christian walk is not easy. We all need, at times, words of encouragement. This may be one of the reasons Jesus sent out His disciples two by two. So they could encourage one another as they spread the good news.

From an article I read over forty years ago on praise and encouragement, I would like to share some insights.

Everyone knows in serving God the importance of praising and worshiping God. It's one of the major principles taught throughout the entire Bible. But I would like to deal with another kind of praise, and that is praising and encouraging one another.

Often when one talks of giving another praise and encouragement, it seems to much of Christianity to be almost sacrilegious to give or even receive it from another. If someone tells you they appreciate how you ministered unto them or that they just love you for who you are, it's often hard to receive it! I hope to show the importance of giving encouragement, and that it's not a sin to receive it.

Given to Jesus, Mark 1:11, "And there came a voice from heaven, saying, Thou art my beloved Son, in whom I am well pleased" (KJV).

It's important that we speak words of approval and endorsement to those who God has brought into our lives. We each need our approval bucket filled from time to time—by either the Lord or other people—so that our personality can flourish.

One of the most difficult and challenging times in my life was when I left an advertising agency I worked at for over twenty years. It was more than my place of employment; these were my best friends and brothers in the Lord as well. My boss was actually the one who led me to the Lord and was the best man at my wedding. Our roots together ran deep. But through various circumstances, we had a parting of the way. I cried. Not having much money, a family to support, and leaving my best friends, it was a dark time. What helped make the difference for me was the encouraging words from my wife. Not words of despair, but *we'll make it together*.

That was over two decades ago now. Through God's grace, I now own an advertising agency, and God turned that dark time into more blessings than I could ever imagine. More important than that, God restored the relationship with those I no longer work with.

The scriptures tell us that God orders our steps and we are most often not even aware of it. We only see what's happening in the moment, but God is orchestrating His purpose in our lives as we walk by faith. Here is an amazing example of that in my life and how we can sometimes get words of encouragement from an unexpected source.

My wife and I purchase rental properties as an investment. Several years ago I was questioning in my mind, "God, are you really in this or am I doing my own thing?" We had recently purchased a group of duplexes in a nearby town from two daughters who were handling their father's estate. In our area, maybe in most, the local newspaper posted real estate transactions naming both buyer and seller. My mom was reading the paper and came across the post of our purchase.

She told me, "I knew the name of the man whose estate it was, but couldn't place it. Then it dawned on me, we lived in Logstown (Aliquippa), your dad was working, your older brother and sister were sick, that fellow was a neighbor who drove me to the hospital to have you."

First of all, I didn't even know we had ever lived in Logstown, which was the town where our church was started and I now serve as associate pastor. It blew me away. I called the daughter who was the executive of the estate and relayed the story. I told her I didn't know what it meant.

She said, "I know what it means: those rentals were good for my dad, and they'll be good for you."

What an encouraging word! I told her, "I claim that." And it has proven to be the case.

If you're familiar with the art of cross-stitch, it illustrates to me God's working in the lives of Christians. My wife has done some cross-stitch; it's a lot of tedious work. And the bigger and more intricate the pattern, the longer it takes to complete.

Let me explain what I mean by God's working. On the top-side is a beautiful pattern that the artist (God) sees. On the bottom side is a lot of loose ends (we see). We know by faith there's a picture being formed, but we can't see the end result. God at times gives us a glimpse, but we'll never see the finished work until we view it from a heavenly view.

I got a little glimpse with the purchase of those duplexes.

The book of Ephesians deals with the dynamics of family relationships between husband and wife, and parents and children.

> Husbands, love your wives, even as Christ also
> loved the church, and gave himself for it.
>
> —Ephesians 5:25, KJV

It's up to the husband to lead the home and included within the responsibility is ministering encouragement and support to his wife and children.

It's not enough to just feel you've expressed your love by your actions (working, bringing home the bacon), but it needs to be said, "Honey, I love you." "Honey, I appreciate you."

Speaking of wives: like everyone, they really need it!

Tell your children you love them. And when your kid goofs up, such as trying to help out mom by cleaning her carpet with Comet, don't drop the bomb automatically, but look through the circumstances and give praise, approval to the motives. Replace condemnation with encouragement and heap it on!

Encouragement in a Bad Situation

It's easy to give encouragement when things are going well, it's another thing to express approval and appreciation when things aren't going too well, but it's even more needed then.

The Story of the Prodigal Son:

> And he said, A certain man had two sons: And the younger of them said to his father, Father, give me the portion of goods that falleth to me. And he divided unto them his living. And not many days after the younger son gathered all together, and took his journey into a far country, and there wasted his substance with riotous living. And when he had spent all, there arose a mighty famine in that land; and he began to be in want. And he went and joined himself to a citizen of that country; and he sent him into his fields to feed swine. And he would fain have filled his belly with the husks that the swine did eat: and no man gave unto him. And when he came to himself, he said, How many hired servants of my father's have bread enough and to spare, and I perish with hunger! I will arise and go to my father, and will say unto him, Father, I have sinned against heaven, and before thee, And am no more worthy to be called thy son: make me as one of thy hired servants. And he arose, and came to his father. But when he was yet a great way off, his father saw him, and had compassion, and ran, and fell on his neck, and kissed him. And the son said unto him, Father, I have

sinned against heaven, and in thy sight, and am no more worthy to be called thy son. But the father said to his servants, Bring forth the best robe, and put it on him; and put a ring on his hand, and shoes on his feet: And bring hither the fatted calf, and kill it; and let us eat, and be merry: For this my son was dead, and is alive again; he was lost, and is found. And they began to be merry. Now his elder son was in the field: and as he came and drew nigh to the house, he heard musick and dancing. And he called one of the servants, and asked what these things meant. And he said unto him, Thy brother is come; and thy father hath killed the fatted calf, because he hath received him safe and sound. And he was angry, and would not go in: therefore came his father out, and intreated him. And he answering said to his father, Lo, these many years do I serve thee, neither transgressed I at any time thy commandment: and yet thou never gavest me a kid, that I might make merry with my friends: But as soon as this thy son was come, which hath devoured thy living with harlots, thou hast killed for him the fatted calf. And he said unto him, Son, thou art ever with me, and all that I have is thine. It was meet that we should make merry, and be glad: for this thy brother was dead, and is alive again; and was lost, and is found.

—Luke 15:11-32, KJV

Both sons blew it: The younger brother went and wasted all the inheritance. The older son stayed home, got bitter in his heart, and

Kenneth H. McGaffic

that bitterness and pride was demonstrated when he was talking to his dad.

The father, though, ministered to both with approval and acceptance. To the younger son, with new clothes, a fatted calf, and a ring ... not with an "I told you so."

> But the father said to his servants, Bring forth the best robe, and put it on him; and put a ring on his hand, and shoes on his feet: And bring hither the fatted calf, and kill it; and let us eat, and be merry: For this my son was dead, and is alive again; he was lost, and is found. And they began to be merry.
>
> —Luke 15:22-24, KJV

To the older son, he took time to explain the situation.

> And he said unto him, Son, thou art ever with me, and all that I have is thine. It was meet that we should make merry, and be glad: for this thy brother was dead, and is alive again; and was lost, and is found.
>
> —Luke 15:31-32, KJV

To be able to give approval and acceptance, we need to see that failure isn't evil, but is merely human. We all do it, and we all need someone to encourage us with words.

A Good Word of Instruction

A good word can also be a word of instruction. The Bible states, "Let the word of Christ dwell in you richly in all wisdom; teaching and admonishing one another in psalms and hymns and spiritual songs, singing with grace in your hearts to the Lord" (Colossians 3:16, KJV).

Consider this, much of Jesus' ministry of teaching and instructing His disciples was not in the temple. Jesus gave words of instruction in a boat, at dinner, walking along the way … you get the point. You don't have to be behind a pulpit to offer a good word of instruction at an appropriate time.

We are constantly being bombarded by messages through all forms of media. Billions of dollars are spent annually in advertising and marketing to sell us something, influence our decisions, or lead us down a path the advertiser wants us to take, many of which do not have our best interest in mind. (To think they don't affect our actions is ludicrous.) We all need good words of instruction and admonishment to keep us on the right way even when, at times, we don't want to hear them.

There is no better counsel than to share the scriptures from a heart of compassion and love. The Bible tells us in Psalm 119:105, "Thy word is a lamp unto my feet and a light unto my path." (KJV).

> Where no counsel is, the people fall: but in the multitude of counsellors there is safety.
>
> —Proverbs 11:14, KJV

Combine these two scriptures and it's easy to see how sharing various scriptures on a subject can be a safe way to bring light to someone who is searching for answers.

If we truly believe that the Bible is God's Word, then when we study the scripture, we discover God's mind in the matter.

When Jesus faced temptation from the devil in the wilderness, He countered the deception of the enemy by quoting Old Testament scriptures. I always thought *if Jesus needed to do that, who do we think we are to try to face all the world throws at us with human reasoning?*

Peter tells us:

> Moreover I will endeavour that ye may be able after my decease to have these things always in remembrance. For we have not followed cunningly devised fables, when we made known unto you the power and coming of our Lord Jesus Christ, but were eyewitnesses of his majesty. For he received from God the Father honour and glory, when there came such a voice to him from the excellent glory, This is my beloved Son, in whom I am well pleased. And this voice which came from heaven we heard, when we were with him in the holy mount. We have also a more sure word of prophecy; whereunto ye do well that ye take heed, as unto a light that shineth in a dark place, until the day dawn, and the day star arise in your hearts: Knowing this first, that no prophecy of the scripture is of any private interpretation. For the prophecy came not in old time by the will of man: but holy men of God spake as they were moved by the Holy Ghost.
>
> —2 Peter 1:15-21, KJV

Verse 19 is referring to the Holy scriptures. I've never experienced what Peter did on the Mount of Transfiguration but I have something even more reliable: God's scripture. Be a student of the Word and be open to share it when the opportunity offers itself, you may be surprised how God uses it to help someone.

How About a
Good Word of Comfort?

When someone who our family knows passes away, my younger daughter says she doesn't like going to the funeral home.

My response is, "Who does? You go to support the grieving family with your presence and words of comfort." Who knows the perfect words to say? I know I don't, but I trust my genuine empathy for their loss will be communicated through what little is said. It's doing good.

Studies have shown, other than the loss of your spouse through death, divorce is a leading cause of stress. With about 40-50 percent of marriages ending in divorce, there's a lot of stress out there. Christians sometimes struggle on what to say to the divorcee, not wanting to condone the break-up of a marriage, but also not wanting to ostracize them. Most times the people feel badly enough; they didn't get married to get divorced. Every situation is different, and every story has two sides. But we need to be willing to express words of comfort to those who were caught up in the pandemic that's destroying families. Unfortunately, when it comes to divorce, you can't unring a bell.

"A bruised reed he will not break; and a smoldering wick he will not snuff out" (Matthew 12:20, NIV). Matthew was quoting a prophecy from Isaiah 42. This spoke of the actions and attitude of

Jesus to those who are damaged, whether spiritually, emotionally, morally, physically, or the popular term today, just dysfunctional.

Jesus said He didn't come to condemn the world but through Him it may be saved. And that salvation touches every area of our lives. We're all "damaged goods," but unlike ordering something online, where we have the opportunity to send it back if it's not perfect when we receive it, we come into this world with a "No Return" label on us. Thankfully, God doesn't throw us away; that's why Jesus came.

When we display the same attitude toward the "bruised reeds and smoldering wicks" we encounter in this life, we're demonstrating the heart of God. We are God's ambassadors. We represent God to this world when we give a good word of comfort in a non-judgmental way. This can be just the same as healing someone's needs.

If you ever wanted to be a doctor, here's your chance to practice medicine. There are hurting patients all around you, take the time to offer a word of comfort. It will do them good and you as well.

CHAPTER 15

Trying to Do Good Can Be Funny

When my youngest daughter was three or four years old, I heard our pastor one Sunday morning on the importance of family. I've always made my family a priority, but after hearing the sermon, I determined I could do better.

It was cold and wintry after church that day, so I decided, why not take my daughter sled riding? What a great way to build family memories. There was a favorite sled riding hill at the local college; it seemed safe enough but just the right height to give my daughter and me a thrill. I parked the car. It seemed to be getting colder so I made sure she was bundled up. We made our way up the hill with her plastic sled, definitely not a Flexible Flyer model, but one that was age-appropriate. I instructed her to not move until I gave her the signal. This was once I made it to the bottom of the hill to catch her. Well, I made my way halfway down the hill when ... *swoosh* ... there she goes! An orange blur with my daughter on it.

Now, there was a landing area to the right at the bottom, but there was also a duck pond to the left. Guess what? She missed the landing area and ended up in the middle of the frozen pond still sitting on the sled. The pond happened to be frozen enough to hold her, but not me. Now if you would have asked her a few years later, she would have said I dove in and swam over to rescue her. Truth be told, I'm not a swimmer, and the pond was only three feet deep, so I trudged through the ice and freezing water to save my little damsel in distress. It definitely wasn't a Baywatch moment.

Obviously, it cut short our sled riding afternoon before it even got started. Well, except for the memorable ride into the pond.

Sometimes, trying to do good can have an unexpected comical ending.

Several years before I was married, the local Red Cross was putting on a drive for blood donations. If I recall correctly, it was for someone we knew who was in need. A close friend and I headed over to the local center to do something good. No big deal, donate blood, a lot of people do it.

In the preliminary interview before we actually donated blood they required a small sample of blood by pricking our fingers. They pricked my finger and down I went, passing out slumping in the chair. My friend was seated next to me and had no trouble at all. Well, it took a long time to live that down. My friend would relate the story every opportunity he had demonstrating how I just dangled in the chair. I don't blame him because if the roles were reversed, I would have done the same thing.

It took me a long time to get over the fear of having blood tests. I used to half-lie that it almost kept me from getting married because at that time, you couldn't get a marriage license without blood work.

Sometimes funny things happen when you try to do good.

One day I loaded up the dishwasher while my wife was getting ready to go to work. Doing good doesn't have to be a big thing. Sometimes simple acts of kindness go a long way.

Taking care of chores in a marriage isn't 50/50, it's 100 percent on both sides, especially if both spouses are working outside the home. Successful marriages are ones whose partners give 100 percent trying to out-serve one another.

Loading up the dishwasher, I noticed we didn't have enough dishwasher soap, so I loaded it with dish soap. Well, it wasn't too long before our kitchen started filling up with soap bubbles. It looked like a scene from *The Three Stooges*, but there weren't three stooges, only one—me. Who knew? My wife came down from upstairs and got a good laugh knowing exactly what I had done.

It wasn't the first time or the last time my attempts to do good at home didn't quite have the desired outcome.

CHAPTER 16

Where Do We Go from Here?

I have a friend, Andrae, who lives in Florida, but before moving to the Sunshine State he was a Canadian farmer. He had a farm with more than 11,000 acres (that's over seventeen square miles) in Saskatchewan. He grew different types of crops, including peas, which he sold to New York City to feed the pigeons in Central Park. (The city paid five times as much for the bird feed than what was paid for human consumption. You figure.) But what caught my attention was he told me he would plant one million dollars' worth of seed in the spring in anticipation of a fall harvest. He said most of the time it worked out, but a couple of times it didn't. One thing was guaranteed: if he never planted the seed, he would have never had a harvest. It took an element of faith on his part to not just plant one year, but to plant year after year with no guarantees.

> He that observeth the wind shall not sow; and he
> that regardeth the clouds shall not reap.
>
> —Ecclesiastes 11:4, KJV

There will always be reasons not to do good because doing good can be hard at times. That's where we need to step out in faith, empowered by the Holy Spirit, looking unto Jesus the author and finisher of our faith (Hebrews 12:2) and "do good," not just one time, but make it a lifestyle. No matter how insignificant your efforts may seem to you, sow that seed of "doing good" and you'll hear at that last day, "Well done my good and faithful servant."

As the lyrics of the song, *Little is Much When God Is in It,* (written by Kittie Suffield) illustrates:

> In the harvest field now ripened
> There's a work for all to do;
> Hark! the voice of God is calling,
> To the harvest calling you.
>
> *Refrain:*
> Little is much when God is in it!
> Labor not for wealth or fame;
> There's a crown, and you can win it,
> If you go in Jesus' name.
>
> In the mad rush of the broad way,
> In the hurry and the strife,
> Tell of Jesus' love and mercy,
> Give to them the Word of Life.
>
> Does the place you're called to labor
> Seem so small and little known?
> It is great if God is in it,
> And He'll not forget His own.
>
> Are you laid aside from service,
> Body worn from toil and care?
> You can still be in the battle,
> In the sacred place of prayer.
>
> When the conflict here is ended

And our race on earth is run,
He will say, if we are faithful,
"Welcome home, My child—well done!"

EPILOGUE

Join Me on the Journey - From the Author

I was raised in Beaver County, a county in Western Pennsylvania. The county was once known for steel mills but now it is known for sports figures from Joe Namath to Mike Ditka and many more.

I grew up in a home where my father worked in a steel mill, and my mother stayed home to care for four children.

My mother took us to a denominational church where we attended Sunday School on a regular basis. I joined the church, got baptized, and was an usher. Sadly to say without really knowing Christ.

Like many of my Dawson Ridge (our housing development) friends, I got in a fair amount of trouble growing up in the sixties. As I look back at the crazy things I did, I believe God even protected me back then.

I always had a void in my life. This emptiness I tried to fill with everything from joining the high school football team (I was the smallest on the team—I say now I was the dummy who held the dummies) to experimenting with alcohol and getting involved in other misguided adventures.

I remember telling my mom one day, "I think you need to take me to a psychiatrist, because I see no meaning in life." She laughed and dismissed it. Little did I know God was setting me up in my search for purpose.

One day when I was a senior in high school, a friend of mine came to school completely changed. The best way I can describe it was like one day he was five-feet-tall and the next day he was seven-feet. There was that much change in his life. I asked him, "What happened to you?"

He told me he had gotten saved at a small mission in my hometown of Beaver. This was during a period in America, and the world, known as the Jesus Movement.

I was desperate for answers. There were things I was doing I knew were wrong, but I couldn't stop. That very day another friend of mine and I headed to the mission. I still recall I was overwhelmed with a fear I would die before I got there.

We walked into the mission and asked two fellows sitting in there, "What's this about people getting saved?" As I look back, it was like a fish jumping into a fisherman's boat. We sat down and they took us through the scriptures, then one of them said, "You look like you're ready to get saved."

I said, "I guess I am."

He led me to a back room where we knelt beside an old couch, and I asked Jesus into my life. At that moment, I knew something happened. I no longer had a fear of dying. I felt like someone got on the inside of me and scrubbed all the dirt out of me. I walked outside, and everything even looked clearer.

My friend who was with me didn't accept Christ that day, but came back the next day and did.

I went home and told my mom, "I got saved."

She said, "Saved from what?"

To be honest, I didn't even know. But that night at the supper table, I was thinking to myself, *a Christian must say grace over his meal.* We didn't do that at our house. When I bowed my head to say grace, I felt physical chains break off of me. I know now, as a new babe in Christ, that I started walking in the little bit of light I

Kenneth H. McGaffic

had, and God honored it and was starting to set me free of things that had me bound.

There's much more, but that's my testimony in a nutshell and how I embarked on the journey to "do good." I would encourage you if you've never asked Jesus Christ to come into your life, why not today? That's where the journey needs to begin.

Doing good doesn't earn us eternal life, it's what Jesus did on the cross that paid for your sins and mine.

God bless you!

—Kenneth H. McGaffic

ABOUT THE AUTHOR

Kenneth McGaffic, along with his wife Linda, are residents of Beaver County, a suburb of Pittsburgh, PA. Ken is the Associate Pastor of Wildwood Chapel, Aliquippa, a non-denominational full gospel church. Ken has been privileged to serve the local church in various capacities over the years, including preaching every Thursday for twenty years at Wildwood Chapel's mid-week service. Ken has gone on numerous short-term missionary construction trips and has taught a seminar for ministers in Honduras, El Salvador, and Guatemala. He was also involved in an outreach ministry at a juvenile detention center and local jail.

Ken is President of McGaffic Advertising, an advertising agency. With his wife, Linda, they are the promoters of Old-Fashioned Christmas in the Woods, a craft festival that draws thousands of attendees from across the country.

Ken and Linda are parents to two beautiful daughters and are blessed to have two marvelous sons-in-law and three precious grandsons.